AFRICAN AMERICAN

BASKETBALL LEGENDS

Kareem Abdul-Jabbar

Charles Barkley

Larry Bird

Wilt Chamberlain

Clyde Drexler

Julius Erving

Patrick Ewing

Anfernee Hardaway

Grant Hill

Magic Johnson

Michael Jordan

Jason Kidd

Reggie Miller

Hakeem Olajuwon

Shaquille O'Neal

Scottie Pippen

David Robinson

Dennis Rodman

CHELSEA HOUSE PUBLISHERS

BASKETBALL LEGENDS

CLYDE DREXLER

J. Kelly

Introduction by
Chuck Daly

CHELSEA HOUSE PUBLISHERS
Philadelphia

Produced by Daniel Bial and Associates
New York, New York

Picture research by Alan Gottlieb
Cover illustration by Earl Parker

First Printing

1 3 5 7 9 8 6 4 2

Library of Congress Cataloging-in-Publication Data

Kelly, J.
    Clyde Drexler / J. Kelly ; introduction by Chuck Daly.
      p. cm. -- (Basketball legends)
    Includes bibiliographical references (p.) and index.
    Summary: Discusses the high-flying Houston
Rockets star and his winning battle for an
NBA championship.
    ISBN 0-7910-4382-7
    1. Drexler, Clyde, 1962- --Juvenile literature. 2. Basketball
players--United States--Biography--Juvenile literature.
[1. Drexler, Clyde, 1962- 2. Basketball players. 3. Afro
-Americans--Biography.] I. Title. II. Series.
GV884.D74K45   1997
796.323'092--dc21
[B]   97-8600
                                            CIP
                                            AC

CONTENTS

BECOMING A
BASKETBALL LEGEND

Chuck Daly

What does it take to be a basketball superstar? Two of the three things it takes are easy to spot. Any great athlete must have excellent skills and tremendous dedication. The third quality needed is much harder to define, or even put in words. Others call it leadership or desire to win, but I'm not sure that explains it fully. This third quality relates to the athlete's thinking process, a certain mentality and work ethic. One can coach athletic skills, and while few superstars need outside influence to help keep them dedicated, it is possible for a coach to offer some well-timed words in order to keep that athlete fully motivated. But a coach can do no more than appeal to a player's will to win; how much that player is then capable of ensuring victory is up to his own internal workings.

In recent times, we have been fortunate to have seen some of the best to play the game. Larry Bird, Magic Johnson, and Michael Jordan had all three components of superstardom in full measure. They brought their teams to numerous championships, and made the players around them better. (They also made their coaches look smart.)

I myself coached a player who belongs in that class, Isiah Thomas, who helped lead the Detroit Pistons to consecutive NBA crowns. Isiah is not tall—he's just over six feet—but he could do whatever he wanted with the ball. And what he wanted to do most was lead and win.

All the players I mentioned above and those whom this series will chronicle are tremendously gifted athletes, but for the most part, you can't play professional basketball at all unless you have excellent skills. And few players get to stay on their team unless they are willing to dedicate themselves to improving their talents even more, learning about their opponents, and finding a way to join with their teammates and win.

It's that third element that separates the good player from the superstar, the memorable players from the legends of the game. Superstars know when to take over the game. If the situation calls for a defensive stop, the superstars stand up and do it. If the situation calls for a key pass, they make it. And if the situation calls for a big shot, they want the ball. They don't want the ball simply because of their own glory or ego. Instead they know—and their teammates know—that they are the ones who can deliver, regardless of the pressure.

The words "legend" and "superstar" are often tossed around without real meaning. Taking a hard look at some of those who truly can be classified as "legends" can provide insight into the things that brought them to that level. All of them developed their legacy over numerous seasons of play, even if certain games will always stand out in the memories of those who saw them. Those games typically featured amazing feats of all-around play. No matter how great the fans thought the superstars were, these players were capable of surprising the fans, their opponents, and occasionally even themselves. The desire to win took over, and with their dedication and athletic skills already in place, they were capable of the most astonishing achievements.

CHUCK DALY, most recently the head coach of the New Jersey Nets, guided the Detroit Pistons to two straight NBA championships, in 1989 and 1990. He earned a gold medal as coach of the 1992 U.S. Olympic basketball team—the so-called "Dream Team"—and was inducted into the Pro Basketball Hall of Fame in 1994.

1

CHAMPION

When Clyde Drexler walked onto the court of the Summit, the Houston Rockets' home court, on June 15, 1995, one game from winning the NBA championship, he was not on unfamiliar territory. He had been there before. At the University of Houston, in his junior year, Drexler and his teammates played North Carolina State but lost in the finals on a last-second shot. While playing for the Portland Trail Blazers, Drexler and his teammates made it to the NBA finals in 1990 only to lose to the Detroit Pistons. The Blazers made a return trip in 1992 facing Michael Jordan and the Bulls, but the result was the same.

Now, though, it finally looked like things would be different. The Rockets were up 3-0 over the Orlando Magic. No team had ever rebounded from a 3-0 deficit. Even if the Rockets didn't

The combination of Shaquille O'Neal (left) and Anfernee Hardaway (right) cannot stop Clyde Drexler as he goes to the hoop for two points in Game 3 of the 1995 NBA championship series.

sweep the Magic, the odds were definitely in their favor. But Clyde Drexler never thought about odds. He would never relax. He knew that until that final buzzer sounded, the game would not be over. Until then, he would never let up.

Drexler had been playing hard throughout the playoffs and was a major reason why the Rockets were on the verge of winning their second consecutive championship. In the first game against the Magic, he scored 23 points and pulled down 11 rebounds. He duplicated his point scoring total for game two and added seven steals to his statistics. His best game, however, was game three. In the Rockets' 106-103 victory, he scored 25 points, grabbed 13 rebounds, and had seven assists. The game was close throughout, and the Magic were trying desperately for a win to hold on. But with 1:46 left in the fourth quarter, Drexler took the ball the length of the court and finished with an emphatic dunk. The play ignited the fans at the Summit and the Rockets had a lead they would never relinquish.

After game three, the other Rockets couldn't help but gush about Drexler's magnificent play. "When Clyde grabs the rebound, puts his head down and takes off, he's like a thoroughbred, and he just makes you run with him," said Rocket guard Mario Elie. "It's like he's 10 years younger, flying by young guys like they're standing still."

"It seemed like every time I looked he was stealing the ball and finishing on the other end of the court with a slam," Hakeem Olajuwon, the Rocket center, said. "Clyde set the tone, he made the difference."

So here he was . . . poised to win a championship. But he never would have been in this position if it were not for a very special Valentine's gift he had received four months earlier. On February 14, Drexler learned he had been traded from the Portland Trail Blazers to the Houston Rockets, the defending NBA champions. He was returning to his hometown, the city where he was a star in high school and college, where his family still lived and ran a barbecue restaurant. Though he had had great years in Portland, the Blazers were in a rebuilding phase and Drexler wanted the chance to win a championship. "I had heard rumors, but I had heard rumors before," Drexler said about the trade. "To get to a club like this was phenomenal. It was the best thing that happened to me in a long time."

Making the trade even sweeter was the opportunity to be reunited with his college teammate, Hakeem Olajuwon. They had been teammates at the University of Houston and on the team that, in 1983, came within a last second shot of winning the national championship.

Before the trade, Olajuwon and Drexler even talked about the possibility of playing together again. "Just thinking about all the things Clyde could do . . . steal passes, run the floor, rebound, shoot . . . made me excited," said Olajuwon. But

Drexler's tough defense helped throttle the Orlando Magic. Here he hounds Anthony Bowie during Game 3 of the finals.

Hakeem the Dream didn't believe his team could get Drexler. Then, just before the trading deadline, Rockets' coach Rudy Tomjanovich asked Olajuwon what he thought about bringing Drexler to Houston. Olajuwon knew they would have to give up a lot to get a player of Drexler's caliber, but he encouraged his coach to do whatever he could to make the trade.

Tomjanovich studied current game films of Drexler and noticed that with his quickness and size, he had the unique ability to post up most guards in the league and was able to pass out of double teams. But what convinced him most was the hunger. "I knew Clyde had been there and come up empty," Tomjanovich said. "I knew he'd do anything to get a ring."

So on Valentine's Day, Tomjanovich pulled the trigger on what he knew would be a controversial trade, sending Otis Thorpe and a first-round draft pick to Portland for Drexler and Tracy Murray.

Even though it was Valentine's Day, not everyone was in love with the deal. Otis Thorpe was a 6'10" power forward, a dominating rebounder, and a very popular member of the 1994 championship team. Trading him for Drexler, who at 32 was an older, and at 6' 7", a smaller, player was questionable. "I hate the deal," Rocket forward, Robert Horry said at the time. "We're trading a power forward for a smaller guy. I don't see it helping us right now."

Others were also skeptical about the trade. They wanted to know who, besides Olajuwon, would pull down rebounds? What would happen to the interior defense? And why would you break up the chemistry of a championship team?

And, at first, the skeptics seemed right. Before the trade, the Rockets were 29-17, after it they were 17-18. But it wasn't really because of Drexler that the team was stumbling. Injuries and illness hit the Rockets hard; the biggest was when Olajuwon was sidelined for a few weeks because of a bout with anemia. While Olajuwon was out, even though the Rockets were losing, it was Drexler who was supplying most of the offense. During the stretch he averaged 21.4 points a game and his passing created better shots for his team-mates while his transition game helped the team's fast break.

Despite the poor record, Drexler won over his new teammates. "Dream went down and Clyde all of a sudden started going for 30, 40 points a game," said Rockets' guard, Mario Elie. "Every-one was like, okay, we're convinced."

"Clyde has only one style of playing: all out," said Olajuwon. "He plays hard all the time, he doesn't know any other way to play, he's always going to do his best. It's one of the things I admired about him all those years."

Even Robert Horry changed his tune. "He is just a regular guy who isn't too interested in the glamorous part of the job," said Horry about Drexler.

Whether they liked the trade or not, it was now history; they had to put it past them. The play-offs were about to begin; time to pull together, to start their quest for another championship.

And pull together they did. In the first and sec-ond rounds of the playoffs, the Rockets staged dramatic comebacks, beating Utah and Phoenix. In the Western Conference finals, they knocked off the David Robinson-led San Antonio Spurs in six games. Once again they were in position to repeat as NBA champs. But now they had to

Announcer Bob Costas (front right) tries not to get hurt as the Rockets celebrate the awarding of the championship trophy. Behind Costas, Drexler and Hakeem Olajuwon (center) celebrate the victory.

do it against the Orlando Magic, the team with the best record in the League. With Shaquille O'Neal, Penny Hardaway, Dennis Scott, and Horace Grant, the Magic were loaded with talent and with the home court advantage, favored to win. Could it be that Drexler would once more come close but never win the big one? And what would he do if he and the Rockets did lose?

"I'm trying desperately to win a championship, but I'm not obsessed with it," Drexler said. "If I never win a title, that won't mar my accomplishments. There have been some great players in the NBA who never won it all. You can't say that Charles Barkley and David Robinson aren't super players. To win a title is the ultimate goal. But this is a team sport. If it doesn't happen, you live with it and go on."

Drexler might have sounded calm and cool, but his teammate Mario Elie believed otherwise. "I've noticed a new fire burning inside him," Elie said. "Clyde wants a ring. He wants a ring bad."

And what would make it even more special would be to win in his hometown. "I'm living this dream of pursuing the ultimate goal back in my hometown," Drexler said.

Drexler's mother, Eunice, summed it up best: "Sure, Clyde wants to win a championship for the Rockets. But no matter what happens, we're all just glad he's back home again. Glad he's so close."

The Rockets won the first three games in the series against the Magic and now only needed one more to wrap it all up. The ultimate goal for Drexler was so close he could practically touch it. Yet he and all his teammates knew that there was still work to be done. "Don't start planning the parade yet," warned Mario Elie.

The fourth game began and, like all the others, was close. The Magic were battling, playing for respect now, showing that they would not give up. But in the fourth quarter, the crowd sensed victory and raised the noise to a thunderous level, helping spur on the Rockets to break the game open. Just before the buzzer sounded, Olajuwon put an explanation point on the season by nailing a 25-foot jumper. The game was over. Rockets 113, Magic 101. A clean four-game sweep. The Rockets were once again NBA champions. Time to celebrate.

In the locker room after the game, the champagne was flowing and Clyde Drexler, who usually drinks just ordinary bottled water, took a sip. For his teammates, including Hakeem Olajuwon, Kenny Smith, Mario Elie, and Sam Cassell, this was an encore presentation; they were all part of the previous year's championship. But for Drexler, it was a first . . . and he was savoring every drop. Now there would be no more doubts . . . no more talk about not winning the big one. Now he was a champion.

2

LEARNING HOW

$\mathbf{A}$s a sophomore in high school, Clyde Drexler was not as obsessed with basketball as were other future hoop stars. He enjoyed playing the game, but, thanks to his mother, Eunice Drexler Scott, he was more concerned with his education. "I was more interested in my studies," Drexler said. "I've always tried to put my education before sports. Basically, as you grow up, you hear older people, like my brothers, and my mom, saying, 'Go to school. Hit those books.' So I did."

Still, Drexler found time for basketball, and when he was 15 years old and 6' 1", he dunked a basketball in a playground game. But not only did Clyde dunk, he dunked on a basket that was a foot higher than regulation. His special ability did not go unnoticed, and when he was a sophomore at Sterling High School in Houston, Texas, the varsity basketball coach invited him to play on the basketball team. Drexler declined

Drexler was the star of his Sterling High School basketball team.

the invitation. He had no time for basketball. There was too much schoolwork to do.

The next year the same coach returned, hoping Drexler, who had shot up to 6′ 4″, would change his mind. "Deep inside I wanted to play, but I still didn't have the time. I told him I was more interested in my studies," said Drexler. "So we had a conference with my mom and persuaded her. And then she persuaded me."

Once everyone was persuaded, Drexler began his basketball education. Sure he knew the playground game. He could dunk and go one-on-one and he was tall and quick, but Drexler understood that he needed much more than natural ability to become a good player. He knew he would have to work hard. He knew he would have to be willing to learn. And he was ready to do both.

The middle child of seven boys and girls, Clyde grew up in a family without a father. His mother supported the family by working as a checker at a local food store. She was the guiding force in the family, but Clyde's first teacher was his older brother, James. The two brothers used to stand on the front porch of their home, in Houston's South Park district, and drill a basketball off the edge of the roof. If you didn't hit the roof at the proper angle, the ball would career away. A direct hit and the ball would return right into the hands of the shooter. The two brothers would play the game endlessly and Drexler credits it with helping him with his jump shot. Of the two brothers, however, it was James who had the sweeter shot. "James had one of these picture-perfect jump shots: high, high arc, perfect form, the whole thing," Clyde recalled.

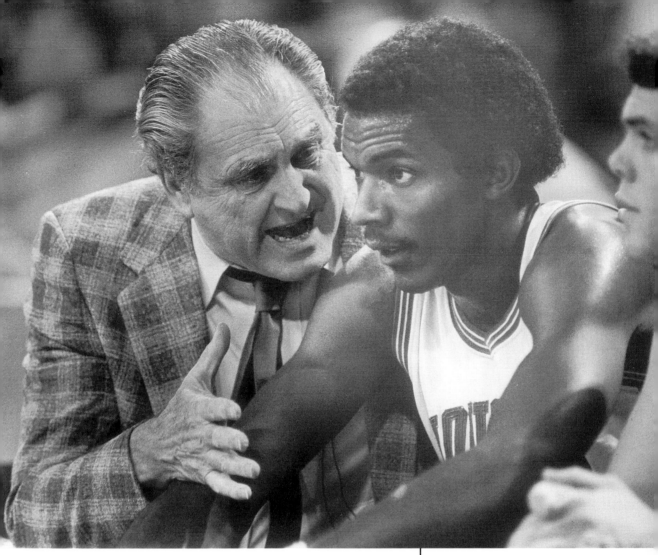

Drexler's reputation in high school, despite all the work on his jump shot, was as a dunker. "Clyde didn't care about shooting," his mother, Eunice, said. "All he wanted to do is dunk."

His first dunk came when he was 15 years old in a game on a playground behind his junior high school. Drexler, who at the time stood 6′ 1″, was guarded by two older, bigger kids. They had him cut off from the basket; the only way he could score was to jump over them. So that was what he did, slamming the ball into the hoop.

Coach Guy Lewis gives some instructions to an intense Clyde Drexler during the 1983 Midwest Regional NCAA championship game. Houston beat Villanova 89-71.

As Drexler later remembered, what was most remarkable was that the hoop was a foot higher than regulation.

Soon, Drexler's jumping ability became legendary in Houston. But not only could he jump, he also had a ballet-like takeoff and an effortless mid-air float on the way to the basket. It was not long after that first dunk that he earned the nickname Clyde "the Glide."

Drexler had great natural skills, but he worked hard to develop them further. He took karate lessons, which helped his coordination. He also began a weightlifting regimen to build muscle.

Jump shot or dunk. Defense or ball handling. Drexler would do whatever was asked of him. In high school he started every game and in the course of the season played every position. By his senior year, he was averaging 17 points, 14 rebounds, and 3 assists per game and was named the team's most valuable player. From a reluctant high school player, Drexler had become a star. Playing mostly center, he led Sterling to the Houston high school finals. The decision he had made two years earlier proved to be one of his best. "Playing high school ball was a great move," Drexler said. "The more I played, the better I played. I've never regretted it."

And at Sterling High, Drexler wasn't the only famous athlete. The school was also the breeding ground for two top women tennis players: Zina Garrison and Lori McNeil. But even though Drexler went to school with the women, he didn't know about their prowess until their senior years. "I sat next to Zina in Spanish class and one night I happened to see her on TV," Drexler said. "She had won some tournament and was being interviewed. The next day I asked her about it and

*Drexler goes in for an
uncontested layup
during the 1983 Final
Four game against
Louisville.*

she said, 'Yeah, I play some tennis.' We became
good friends after that."

Garrison and McNeil spurred Drexler's interest in playing tennis. In recent years, he has
spent a lot of time during the off-season on a
different sort of court. "I get free lessons as long
as they're in town," said Drexler. "If they want
some tips on basketball, I help out."

But tennis would never make Drexler a star. Basketball would. Even though his reputation as a hoopster was growing, Drexler was only recruited by three major colleges: Texas Tech, New Mexico State, and the University of Houston. A friend and Houston high school rival, Michael Young, who was one of the top recruits in Texas, decided to attend the University of Houston. Young told University of Houston basketball coach Guy V. Lewis that the best player he had played against was Clyde Drexler. That was enough to convince Lewis to sign Drexler, and in the fall of 1980, Drexler enrolled at the University of Houston.

Guy Lewis had been the coach at Houston for over 20 years. The basketball program at the school had an excellent reputation. Houston was where former college and NBA great Elvin Hayes had played. Lewis was tough with his freshman, rarely allowing them to start, but for the 1980-81 season, there were two exceptions: Michael Young and Clyde Drexler.

It was only Drexler's third year of organized ball and he was still learning the game and continuing to improve. "I didn't realize I was gonna be any good until my freshman year," Drexler said. "I kept working hard. I was a gym rat. People were telling me: 'Hey, you're pretty good.'"

In his freshman year, Drexler averaged 11.9 points per game, but it was in rebounding where he really excelled. In one game he had 17 rebounds, while in four other games he grabbed 16 boards. For the year, he averaged 10.5 rebounds per game and was the number two rebounder in the Southwest Conference. His fine play earned him the honor of 1981 Newcomer of the Year in the Southwest Conference (SWC) as well as second team All-SWC. A reporter wrote that Clyde's moves on the court were similar to those of the great Julius Erving. For Drexler, being compared to his childhood hero, Dr. J., was the highest compliment he could imagine.

While Drexler continued to learn, Lewis was assembling a championship team at Houston. Joining Drexler was another leaper named Larry Micheaux. And then there was a seven footer from the African nation of Nigeria who had recently enrolled at the school. He could run the floor like a smaller guard, leap like a forward, and he was an instinctive shot blocker. His basketball ability was raw, but his potential was enormous. His name was Hakeem (then spelled Akeem) Olajuwon.

Drexler, in his sophomore season, began to establish himself as a star. His shooting average went up to 15.2 a game while his rebounding equaled the previous year's at 10.5. But scoring and rebounding weren't the only elements of his game that stood out; he also had lightning quick hands, resulting in 97 steals for the year. He was becoming the complete player.

In 1982, Young, Micheaux, Olajuwon, and Drexler lost to Arkansas in the SWC championship game, but were picked as an unranked team to enter the NCAA tournament. No one gave them much of a chance to go very far in the tournament, but coach Lewis had other ideas. "I've been going to the Final Four the past 14 years by myself," Coach Lewis told the team on the eve of the tournament. "This year I'd like to bring my team."

In the first two games, the Cougars beat Alcorn State and Tulsa. In the third game, Houston was matched up with the highly-ranked Tigers of the

*Drexler and Olajuwon (right)
were the key members in
Houston's famed "Phi Slama
Jama" fraternity.*

University of Missouri. The Cougars upset the
Tigers and then beat Boston College to make it
to the Final Four for the first time since 1968 . . .
when Elvin Hayes was on the team.

In the Final Four semi-final game, Houston
was matched against number-one ranked North
Carolina, a team featuring three future NBA
stars: James Worthy, Sam Perkins, and the great

Michael Jordan. The Tar Heels were regulars in the Final Four, but their coach, Dean Smith, had never won a championship. The game was played in front of over 30,000 spectators in New Orleans' Superdome. And as it turned out, North Carolina was just too good for the Cougars, beating them 68-63 and then going on to defeat Georgetown for the championship two days later.

The tournament brought the best out of Drexler. In five tournament games, he shot 59.3 percent, averaged 16 points a game, and added 8.2 rebounds, two assists, and three steals a game. He also led the NCAA tournament in total rebounds with 41. Some of the awards he received after the season included honorable mention All-American honors from *The Sporting News*, All-SWC, and, once again, team MVP.

The following year everything seemed to come together, not only for Drexler, but for the Houston Cougars. They lost some tough games early but then went on a streak in January, February, and March where they won 22 games in a row. All of the Cougar hoopsters had great leaping ability. They literally dunked teams to defeat. In their honor, a fraternity at Houston was formed called "Phi Slama Jama," a pun on the renowned academic fraternity, Phi Beta Kappa. No one dunked with more flair than Drexler.

With the presence of Olajuwon, Drexler's rebounding average in 1982-83 dropped to 8.8 per game, but his scoring remained a consistent 15.2. In one game against SWC rival Baylor he knocked down 29 points, while against Syracuse University, the Big East power, he scored 28. In the same game against Syracuse, Drexler set a career and school record with 11 steals. By the end of the season, Drexler had broken his own record for steals (97), by swiping 113. He also became the only player in Houston Cougar history to score at least 1,000 points, pull down over 900 boards, and dish out 300 assists.

But records only look good on paper. Drexler and the other members of Phi Slama Jama wanted a national championship. They were labeled as a team with enormous physical skills but lacking fundamentals. Because of this, sportswriters predicted an early exit for the Cougars; they would not survive against better drilled teams. They wanted to prove their critics wrong. To show the country that they were more than just dunking machines. And they did.

In the tournament they beat Maryland, Memphis State, and Villanova to make the trip to the Final Four once again. This time the location was Albuquerque, New Mexico, and in the semifinal game, they were pitted against the Louisville Cardinals. It was a dream matchup. The Doctors of Dunk, as the Cardinals were known, against Phi Slama Jama. But the game turned out to be no contest. Houston won 94-81.

The surprise opponent in the final was the North Carolina State Wolfpack, a team that had underachieved all season. They were coming together in the Tournament, however, and Houston, though favored, was wary. In the game, the Wolfpack, with their big front line, neutralized Houston's quickness and slowed the game to their tempo. Still, it was close throughout. With the game tied and less then five seconds to go, N.C. State's Dereck Whittenberg threw up a desperation shot that fell short, but, unbelievably, found itself in the hands of the Wolfpack's Lorenzo Charles who quickly put in a lay-up to win the game at the buzzer.

It was a dramatic, memorable ending with the Wolfpack's coach, Jim Valvano, gleefully running onto the court to congratulate his players. The Cougars, on the other hand, were stunned. How could it be? How did they lose? For Drexler, Olajuwon, and the others it was a hurt that wouldn't soon go away.

After the sting of defeat slowly faded, it was time for Drexler to assess his future. He had one more year of college eligibility left, but NBA scouts were showing more than just a little interest in him. The Houston Rockets had the first and third picks in the draft. Maybe, if he came out, they would pick the hometown hero. To play in the NBA had been one of Drexler's childhood dreams. To play in his hometown would be even sweeter. His mother wanted him to get his degree, but left the decision up to him. It was a tough one, but he decided to forgo his senior season and enter the draft.

When he announced his decision, Drexler thanked the University and praised his coach. "To me, Guy Lewis was a great teacher," Drexler said. "He started all this for me. And I'll tell you, if I had to do it all over again. I'd go to UH again without a doubt. It was a great experience."

3

TRAIL BLAZING

On a June day in 1983, Clyde Drexler was waiting by the phone to learn about his future. It was NBA draft day. Drexler was hoping to stay right at home in Houston, but with the first pick in the draft, the Rockets chose the 7' 4" Ralph Sampson. Drexler's heart raced again when the Rockets were called to make the third pick. But, once more, he was ignored; instead, the Rockets opted for Louisville forward Rodney McCray. "I was upset," Drexler said. "I came out a year early with the idea that the Rockets would grab me. When they didn't, I was disappointed."

All right, so he wouldn't be playing in Houston. He would definitely be picked soon . . . maybe Utah . . . or Chicago . . . or Dallas. The phone, however, did not ring, and Drexler began to get very anxious. "I could've stayed in school another year and gone higher in next year's

Dudley Bradley of the New Jersey Nets stops short and referee Lee Jones looks as if he's taking cover, but Drexler is under control as he looks to pass to a teammate before going out of bounds.

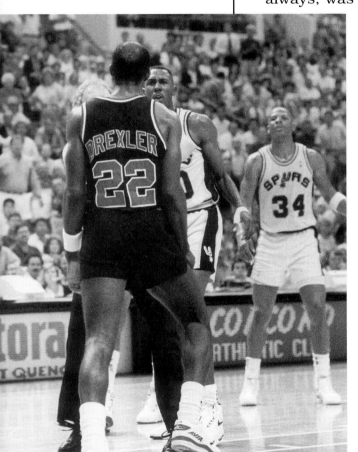

Drexler's temper occasionally got the better of him. Here he faces off against Willie Anderson of the San Antonio Spurs before being ejected by the referee.

draft," he thought, as the picks mounted. Finally, with the 14th pick, the Portland Trail Blazers called his name.

He would be playing in Oregon. It was a long way from home, but it would be a new, possibly very exciting experience. And his mother, as always, was there to support him. "I'm a firm believer that whatever happens, happens for the better," Eunice Drexler Scott said. Drexler told himself that he would make the best of the situation and never look back.

The Portland Trail Blazers came into the NBA in 1970 and for the first few years floundered in the obscurity of the Pacific Northwest. But in 1977, the team, lead by Bill Walton, Maurice Lucas, Dave Twardzik, and Lionel Hollins, came out of nowhere to win the hearts of not only the Portland community but of the country when they defeated the powerful Philadelphia 76ers to capture the NBA crown.

"Blazermania" affected most people in Oregon as well as parts of California, Washington, and even Idaho and Wyoming. But the magic of the 1977 season was never duplicated. Bill Walton, the seven-footer who was supposed to be the next Kareem Abdul-Jabbar, suffered debilitating injuries. Lucas, the quintessential power forward, was traded. The nucleus of the team fell apart.

In 1983, Drexler was coming to a team that could only be described as mediocre. They had never regained the edge they had had in the 1970s, though their fanatical following continued. Although Memorial Coliseum is currently the smallest pro basketball stadium—it seats fewer than 13,000 people (whereas the Charlotte Coliseum seats over 23,000 people)—it is regularly sold out and there is always pressure to win. Portland is a small media market, but no other professional major league sports have their home in Oregon. The Blazers thus dominate the local sports scene. It can be a fantastic place to play . . . or a very tough one. It all depends on how well the team handles the pressure.

In his first season with the Blazers, Drexler played in all 82 games but only averaged 17.2 minutes per game. He was treated as a raw rookie; he'd have to prove himself before he was allowed to see more action. The Blazers finished with a 48-34 record in Drexler's first season and lost to the Phoenix Suns in five games in the first round of the playoffs. For the 1983-84 season, Drexler averaged 7.7 points per game. It would be the last time his scoring average would be in the single digits.

One of the problems for Blazer head coach Jack Ramsey was to find a position that best suited Drexler's skills. At 6′ 7″, Drexler had the height and leaping ability to play forward. But he also had the speed and ball-handling ability to play guard. Ramsey eventually saw enough of intraconference rival Earvin "Magic" Johnson of the Los Angeles Lakers to know that being tall was no reason not to play guard. Johnson at 6′ 9″ could dribble and distribute the ball as well as anyone, and his extra height made it extra difficult for defenders to block his shots. Ramsey started to pencil Drexler in the lineup most often as a guard. Drexler still stayed active on the boards rebounding and often led the Blazers' fast break.

In the 1984-85 season, hints of the superstar to come were becoming evident. Drexler started 42 games for the Blazers and his minutes increased dramatically from his rookie season. As a result, his scoring average more than doubled to 17.2 points per game. In one game against the San Antonio Spurs, Drexler scored 37 points, while in another against the Los Angeles Lakers, he handed out 13 assists. "I knew it would happen for me once I got the minutes," Drexler said. "The first night as a starter, I got over 30 minutes and had 25 points and 17 rebounds. It just carried on from there."

The Blazers finished with a 42-40 record in 1984-85 and beat the Dallas Mavericks in the first round of the playoffs. In the second round, the Blazers were defeated in five games by the Los Angeles Lakers, who went on to win the NBA championship that season.

In Drexler's third season, he began a string of consecutive All-Star game appearances. In the 1986 game, he scored 10 points in 15 minutes. For the season, he averaged 18.5 points per game along with 2.6 steals, good enough to place him third in the league. Portland once again made the playoffs, but lost in the first round to the Denver Nuggets.

By now, any disappointment he had had with being drafted by Portland and not Houston was long gone. "I'm glad I went off to play in Portland," he said at the time. "It has expanded my world. I'm meeting new people and living in a beautiful part of the country."

And Portland was equally glad. They had a player who was starting to be considered among

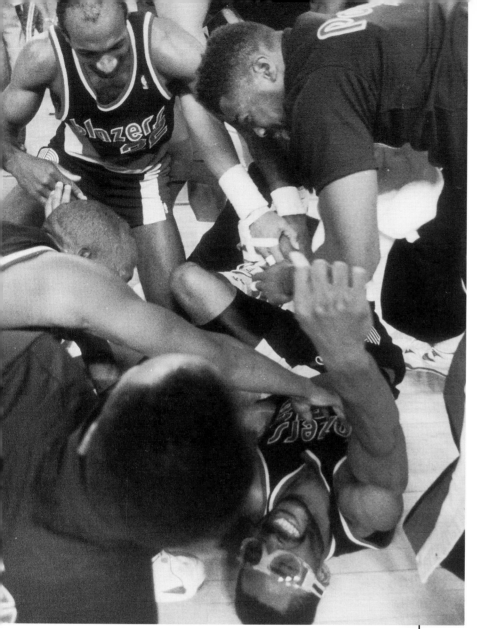

Drexler had infrequent opportunities to celebrate while with the Portland Trail Blazers. But in 1990, Drexler (upper left) and Buck Williams (on the floor) rejoiced after beating the Phoenix Suns to win the Western Conference title.

the NBA's elite. Experts talked about him in the same breath as Magic Johnson, Larry Bird, and Michael Jordan. In the 1986-87 season, Drexler, Bird, and Magic were the only players in the league to average more than 21 points, 6 assists, and 6 rebounds per game.

Not only was Drexler doing it on the court, he was also contributing off-court. In the off-season, back home in Houston, he started a basketball camp for inner-city kids where, along with learning hoop skills, Houston police officers and Drexler himself drilled them about staying away from drugs and crime. "The more they know about the dangers of drugs, the less likely they are to do it," Drexler said of his work. "I figure, educate them when they're young, and maybe you can save a few."

For his work, Drexler was honored by then President Reagan and the First Lady. "It was a pleasure to meet the President and Mrs. Reagan," Drexler said of the experience. "He's a busy guy, but it was a thrill to meet him."

Drexler's work with kids earned him an invitation to the White House in 1986. Here he shakes hands with President Sarney of Brazil as President Ronald Reagan looks on.

In the Fall of 1987, Drexler was beginning his sixth year in the league. By the spring of 1988, when the season was over, he had firmly established himself as one of the NBA's premier players. He boosted his scoring average to 27.0 points per game and established a Portland Trail Blazer record by scoring 2,185 points. He was also named Player of the Week three times and was voted into the All-Star game where he scored 12 points in just 15 minutes of action.

The next year, Drexler equaled his previous year's scoring average of 27.0 points per game. In one thrilling overtime game against the Sacramento Kings he tossed in a career high 50 points. An All Star once again, Drexler played 25 minutes in the midseason classic and scored 14 points along with 12 rebounds. He also entered the Slam-Dunk contest, held annually at the All-Star game. He thrilled the crowd with some amazingly acrobatic moves, but finished second to Kenny Walker of the New York Knicks for the championship. Some say that Drexler really deserved the championship, but Walker won it as a sympathy vote because of the recent death of his father.

And though he was learning the finer aspects of the game, working on his outside shot, ball handling, and defensive skills, Drexler's reputation was that of a slam dunk artist. With a vertical leap measured at 43 inches, Drexler probably could have excelled as an Olympic high jumper. And, on the basketball court, whenever the opportunity arose, he would take off, his muscular 6' 7" frame gliding in the air, and slam one down. "It pumps me up to dunk," Drexler said. "And it's a high percentage shot." Perhaps the greatest example of Drexler's leaping ability occurred in 1989 when he set a Portland record by dunking on an 11' 1" basket.

His exuberance, however, has not always been wise. Since coming into the NBA, he has been knocked unconscious twice in dunk attempts. "That's the only bad thing," Drexler admitted. "There's no room for cowardice in basketball. You can't be intimidated by some rim."

While Drexler's star was rising, the Blazers were starting to come together as a team. Before the 1989-90 season, they traded for All-Star forward Buck Williams who, along with Drexler, Jerome Kersey, Kevin Duckworth, Terry Porter, and sixth man Cliff Robinson, formed the nucleus of a dominating team. With talent around him, Drexler made a bold prediction. "I think we have a championship-caliber team, and we're going to get there," he said before the season.

Drexler's words turned out to be prophetic. After four years of being eliminated in the first round of the playoffs, the Blazers finally got over the hump, defeating the San Antonio Spurs in seven games and then, in the Western Conference Finals, taking the Phoenix Suns in six. The Blazers were going to the NBA Finals, and Drexler credited team chemistry and depth for their success. "That's why we're still playing," he said. "If you have only one or two guys, teams can take them away. If the other guys don't respond, you go home. Our team structure is different, and I wouldn't have it any other way. It was just a golden moment for us as a team. And we seized the moment."

The moment, however, did not last. The Blazers' opponent in the finals was the reigning NBA champion, the Detroit Pistons. The "Bad Boys" featured Isiah Thomas, Dennis Rodman, Bill Laimbeer, and Joe Dumars. They were known for their tough, almost bullying style of play. The Blazers knew they were in for a physical series and, as it turned out, it was too physical. The Pistons beat the Blazers in five games to repeat as champions.

Losing in the finals was a bitter end to another stellar year for Drexler. For the season, he averaged 23.3 points, 6.9 rebounds, and 5.9 assists. And earlier in the 1989-90 campaign, he had surpassed the 10,000 point mark for his career. In the 21 playoff games that year, Drexler averaged 21.4 points and 7.2 rebounds. His best game was the Blazers' only win in the Finals, where he scored 33 points, including two clutch free throws in overtime for the victory.

The next year, the Blazers had hopes of returning to the NBA finals, but this time they wanted to walk away winners. They stormed through the regular season, finishing with a magnificent 63-19 record. They won the first two rounds of the playoffs but were denied a trip to the Championship round by the Los Angeles Lakers, who defeated them in the Western Conference Finals.

Again, in the 1990-91 season, Drexler was voted into the All-Star game and, in the game, scored 12 points in 19 minutes. This time, instead of entering the Slam Dunk Championship as usual, he displayed his versatility by entering the Long Distance Shootout contest. For the season, he averaged 21.5 points, 6.7 rebounds, and 6.0 assists and was a member of the All-NBA Second Team.

Despite all the accolades, Drexler never stopped working on his game. He was entering the prime of his career and was driven to be the best. "My edge isn't my talent; it's the fact I'm always in shape. I've always got keys to the gym," he said.

He also credited his willingness to continue to learn. To keep an open mind and try to expand his game. "I've tried to make strides in the game, but there are things that happen with experience," Drexler said. "You get more experience, and you make better decisions."

All that hard work was beginning to pay off for him. He was considered one of the top ten players in the game. Individual awards, he conceded, were nice, but he was still without a championship. It was the one missing link in what, so far, had already been a tremendous career.

4

PRIME YEARS

Entering the 1991-92 season, Clyde Drexler was 29 years old. He had been to two NCAA Final Fours and one NBA Final. He had been to five NBA All-Star games and was considered one of the game's premier players. But Drexler had the misfortune of excelling in a time when other superstars were hogging the headlines. It was a golden era in basketball. There were greats such as Larry Bird, Magic Johnson, Michael Jordan, Charles Barkley, and Isiah Thomas, who were charismatic on and off the court. Drexler believed he was in their class, and his statistics backed him up; he just did not get the headlines the others did.

Drexler's teammate, Terry Porter, believed it was the lack of a championship. "When they compare great players, they compare rings,"

Showing off his Michael Jordan pose, a frustrated Clyde Drexler waits for the action to resume during the 1992 NBA Finals. The real Michael Jordan and the Chicago Bulls beat the Trail Blazers in this first game of the championships by a margin of 33 points.

Porter said. "That's why Russell is considered better than Chamberlain. Unfair or not, to be considered a really great player, Clyde needs a ring."

In December 1988, Drexler married Gaynell Floyd at the St. Charles Avenue Baptist Church in New Orleans.

Rick Adelman, Drexler's coach at Portland at the time, pointed toward the lack of media attention as the main factor in his star player not getting the credit he deserved. "Portland doesn't get the exposure of other clubs," Adelman said. "People don't see enough of what he can do and the way he can play and pass. The league has chosen to showcase certain players, and Clyde isn't one of them."

Maybe it was Drexler himself who shunned the attention. "I'm just uncomfortable talking about myself or my family," said Drexler, who had married Gaynell Floyd, a lawyer, three years earlier and had two children.

"The guy [Drexler] is extremely thoughtful and honest. But he'd rather protect his privacy," said Geoff Petrie, senior vice president and director of operations for the Blazers.

Then there was the misconception that he was a wild, undisciplined, selfish player. It was the label that bugged Drexler the most.

When he came into the league from the University of Houston, a member of the Phi Slama Jama fraternity, people thought all he could do was run and dunk. That he just played on his "God-given" athletic ability alone. "God-given, my butt," Drexler said, adamantly. "I resented people thinking that way. You've got to work your butt off when you're on the court. Nothing comes easy."

And, like most young players, his first years in the league were a learning experience. He admitted to making mistakes, but did not feel he was a wild player. "I don't think my game was very wild," Drexler said. "I think everybody makes mistakes. Because I was a faster-paced player and played to my strengths, that could be considered wild. If you never make an effort to try anything, you're never going to make mistakes. I had to work and play very hard to overcome the stereotype of being a wild player. It was purely a perception."

But that was when he was young and inexperienced. Now, at 29, he believed he had matured and that the labels given to him when he was younger should be dropped. "I've tried to make strides to my game, but those are things that happen with experience," Drexler said. "I think I'm more in control and I think I've learned over the years to calm my game down and slow it down. There's a right time to do certain things, and you've just got to pick your time."

In his fight for respect, Drexler had his supporters, including his teammates. "I used to think he was selfish," Blazer forward, Buck Williams said. "I realized he's a fine passer, very unselfish. He's been misread tremendously."

The opposition had also taken notice. "I think he is a smarter player, more under control," said

Phoenix Suns' President, Jerry Colangelo. Jeff Malone, a guard for the Utah Jazz, agreed: "He does so many things well that when you put him under control, how do you stop him?"

Still, gaining the respect of his peers and the rest of the country came slowly for Drexler and, though he never seemed to care, that lack of recognition really hurt when he was left off the 1992 Olympic U.S. Men's basketball Dream Team.

"It's a travesty," said Blazer coach Rick Adelman about the slight.

"I was hurt," admitted Drexler at the time, "but I quickly forgot about it. There is no explanation for it, so why worry about it."

Drexler might have forgotten about it, but during the 1991-92 season, he set out to prove all the doubters wrong. Before the season, as the senior player on the Blazers, he named himself captain of the team. "I just wanted to be able to talk to the referees," joked Drexler.

But Geoff Petrie saw the move as something other than a joke. "It was a statement on his part," the Blazer guard said. "But it was also a reflection of his growth. He has become someone who sees the bigger picture. A lot of players have a narrow perspective when they first come into the league. He's evolved beyond that now, to where he is very comfortable with his place in the world. He's secure as to where he is as a player and a person."

Helping Drexler to evolve and become more secure with himself was his wife Gaynell. Both Clyde and Gaynell enjoyed traveling around the world and shared an interest in learning foreign languages. Gaynell also spurred Clyde to learn about ballet and to take up playing the piano.

"Each year I try to expand my learning experience by taking on a new challenge," Drexler said. "I don't want to become stagnant as a person."

And part of his evolution as a person meant giving back to the community that supported him. He believed that he had a responsibility, that he was a role model and kids looked up to him just as he had looked up to athletes when he was younger. "I loved Julius Erving and Willie Mays," Drexler said. "They were nice guys. I also liked Walt Frazier [of the New York Knicks], mainly because his nickname was Clyde, but he was also a very classy guy. And [tennis legend] Arthur Ashe. What can you say? He went out there and took a stand when there was no one who did it before him to emulate."

In Portland, Drexler headed a program that offered incentives to kids who excel in school. "That gave me a lot of pleasure," Drexler said. "I think that's part of your civic responsibility. I think as an athlete you are a role model. If you're put on that pedestal, you should make it a positive experience."

For the Trail Blazers, the 1991-92 season was also a very positive experience. The team finished with a 57-25 record, the best record in the Western Conference. Drexler had his best year as a pro. He averaged 25.0 points, 6.6 rebounds, and 6.7 assists per game. He was selected as a starter for the All-Star game in Orlando, Florida, and, with 22 points, 9 rebounds, 6 assists, and 2 blocked shots in just 28 minutes of action, was runner-up for MVP to Magic Johnson, who made a brief comeback from retirement to play in the game. After the season, he was named for the first time to the first team All-NBA squad and was second only to Michael Jordan in the

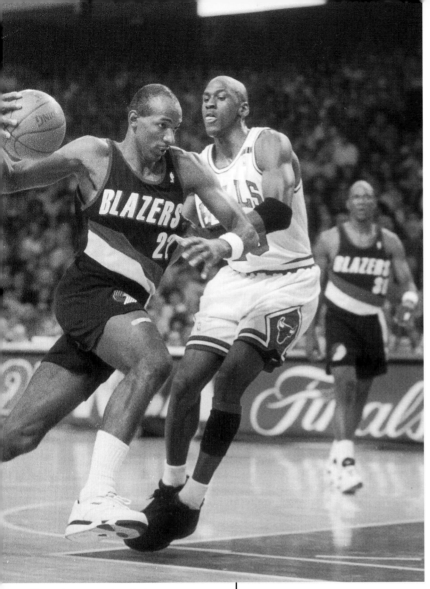

Drexler tries to drive on Michael Jordan during the 1992 NBA Finals. The Bulls were too good for the Trail Blazers, however, and won the series in six games.

voting for the league MVP award.

"I think this season, more so than in the past, Clyde is the reason the Blazers have the best record," said Seattle SuperSonic President, Bob Whitsitt. "He's carrying a bigger load than ever before, and they're still the team to beat out here."

"Like all great players, Clyde's gotten better every year," said Geoff Petrie. "A great example of that is that we asked more of him this year, putting him in the low post, which was not something we had in our offense a year ago. Now, he has become a very effective, creative low-post player."

Drexler's superb play continued after the regular season and into the playoffs. In the first round, in a game against the Lakers, he scored 42 points, the most ever by a Blazer in a postseason game. The Blazers went on to beat the Lakers and Phoenix, and then, in six games, they defeated the Utah Jazz to advance to the NBA finals for the second time in three years. Their opposition would be Michael Jordan and the Chicago Bulls, the defending NBA champs. And with the matchup, the inevitable Jordan/Drexler comparisons commenced.

Beginning the debate was Jordan's coach at Chicago, Phil Jackson. "If there is anyone in this game who comes close to Michael in terms of talent, it's Clyde Drexler," Jackson said.

"Clyde is right there next to Michael when it comes to spectacularism," Phoenix Suns' coach, Cotton Fitzsimmons said. "Without Michael, we'd all be talking about Clyde and the fabulous things he does."

"He's not quite Jordan, but he has the same tough, athletic body," Utah Jazz coach, Jerry Sloan said.

Kevin Edwards, a guard on the Miami Heat, believed Drexler could hold his own against Jordan. "I think he matches up well with Michael," Edwards said. "If Michael concentrates too much on the offensive end, Clyde will come down and light him up at the other end."

"They both do the same things for their teams—score, rebound, pass the ball, make steals, block shots, dominate," said Clyde's brother, James. "How can you say one's better than the other?"

"Nobody understands how good Clyde really is because he doesn't have all the drama behind him that Michael does," said John Lucas, a former NBA guard himself. "When Michael goes to the basket, you sit there and say, 'Oooh.' When Clyde goes to the basket, you say, 'Boy, that's nice.' He just has a more reserved air about him. He makes it look simple."

Drexler was thrilled by the comparison, but had other things on his mind. "I think it's an honor to be compared to Michael," Drexler said, "but the real satisfaction comes in seeing how well your team does. For me, that's the ultimate."

The ultimate, however, did not come true. The Bulls were already the world champions, having defeated the Los Angeles Lakers in the finals the previous year. After splitting the first four games of the series, the Bulls took the advantage by beating the Blazers in Game 5 in Portland. Heading back to Chicago with a 3-2 lead, many fans expected the Blazers to give up.

But the Blazers showed their spirit, manufacturing a 15-point lead, 79-64, as the third quarter expired. The Bulls went on a 14-2 run to start the last quarter, and the two Chicago superstars, Jordan and Scottie Pippen, scored the Bulls' last 19 points to give them a 97-93 victory. Chicago had its second consecutive world championship, and they would defend their title successfully again the following year, to make them the first three-time winners since the Boston Celtics ran off an unprecedented nine titles from 1957 to 1965.

Drexler, Karl Malone, and John Stockton (left to right) applaud after being given their gold medals at the 1992 Olympics.

In the series, Drexler certainly held his own, averaging 24.8 points, 7.8 rebounds, and 5.3 assists per game, but it was another tough end to a glorious season. What helped brighten the year for Drexler was, after the earlier snub, being named as a supplemental addition to the U.S. men's basketball Dream Team. He would be going to Barcelona and playing with the best in the world after all.

"After being left off the first time, I wasn't expecting anything," Drexler said. "I wasn't very happy for a while after not being named to the original team. And then I had to answer six months of questions which was a distraction. It's a pleasure to be on the team and the end of a long ordeal."

Modest and low-key as always, Drexler gave credit to others for his Olympic induction. "This represents everything I've learned," Drexler said. "It's because of all my friends, my family, the people of Houston, the city of Portland, and Guy V. Lewis that I'm in the Olympics."

Looking around at his teammates on the Dream Team, Charles Barkley, Patrick Ewing, Karl Malone, John Stockton, Larry Bird, Michael Jordan, Scottie Pippen, and Magic Johnson, Drexler was overwhelmed. "When you have guys of this magnitude, it's almost unbelievable how much is on this team," Drexler said. "When my career is over, the highlight would be an NBA title. But right after that, it would be an Olympic gold medal."

Well, it didn't take long to get that gold medal. The Dream Team annihilated all opposition and easily captured the gold in Barcelona, Spain.

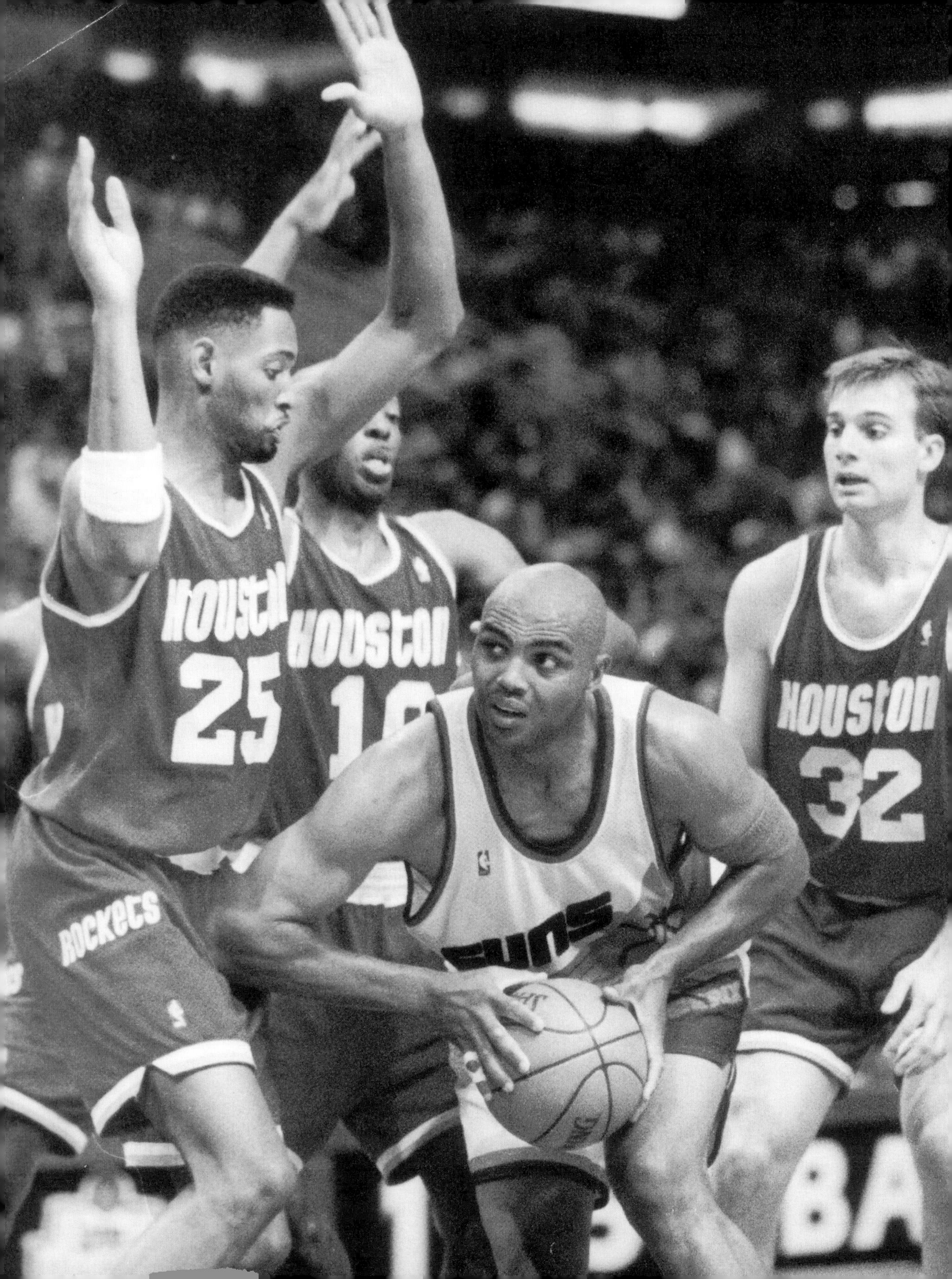
HOUSTON
25
HOUSTON
HOUSTON
32
ROCKETS
SUNS

5
GOING HOME

The great players, according to Geoff Petrie, have their best years between the ages of 28 and 32. "That's when the intellectual side . . . the understanding of how the game is played . . . combines with the physical talent," said Petrie. And Clyde Drexler, at 30, was at the top of his game in 1992. But there is a danger once a player passes his 30th birthday. The body wears down a little easier. The aches hurt longer. And the pains do not heal as fast. Injuries become a way of life.

So it was with Clyde Drexler for the 1992-93 season. For the first time in his career, he was nagged by injuries, spending three separate stints on the injured list. Some of his numerous ail-

The Houston Rockets won the sudden-death Western Conference semi-final game against the Phoenix Suns in 1995 by 115-114. Charles Barkley tried to lead the Suns to a victory, here coming up against (left to right) Robert Horry, Sam Cassell, and Pete Chilcutt. Ironically, Barkley was traded to the Rockets just over a year later for Horry and Cassell.

Drexler glides to the basket as Orlando's Penny Hardaway gets out of the way during the 1995 NBA Finals.

ments included a strained hamstring and a sore right knee. He missed 33 regular season games, compared to just six the previous season, and his points per game average was under 20 for the first time in six years. He finished with a 19.9 average and the Blazers were 30-19 with Drexler in the lineup and 21-12 without him.

Once again he was voted to start in the All-Star Game, but, reflecting the type of season it was, he only scored 2 points in 11 minutes of play. The disappointing season ended when the Blazers, who had come so close to a championship in 1992, were knocked out in the first round of the playoffs by the San Antonio Spurs.

The following season, though he was not as hard hit by injuries as the previous year, Drexler was again hobbled, this time by a sprained left ankle that caused him to miss 14 games. Despite the injuries, Drexler's popularity was on the rise; people were beginning to appreciate his vast talents, and he was second in All-Star votes behind Charles Barkley.

In the 1993-94 season, Drexler, for the first time in seven years, did not lead the Blazers in scoring. His points per game average of 19.2 was second to Cliff Robinson's 20.1. A highlight of the season for Drexler was surpassing Bill Walton to become Portland's all-time rebounding leader. The Blazers finished with a 47-35 record and were matched against the Houston Rockets in the first round of the playoffs. The Blazers played them tough, and Drexler rose to the occasion, averaging 21.0 points, 10.0 rebounds, and 5.5 assists per game in the series, but the Rockets, who went on to win the NBA championship, were just too strong for the Blazers.

With two consecutive years of persistent injuries behind him, people were beginning to wonder if it wasn't the end for Clyde Drexler. Maybe all that running and dunking was finally taking a toll on his body? Maybe he couldn't withstand the punishment the grueling, 82-game NBA season dishes out? Could it be that he was at the twilight of a very fine career?

There were changes in Portland after the 1993-94 season. A new coach, P. J. Carlesimo, and president, Bob Whitsitt, took over with rebuilding in mind. They knew they had a superstar in Drexler, but an aging, and suddenly injury-prone one. Their dilemma was to build a new team around him or deal him for younger, up-and-coming players. Either way, the situation was not a good one for Drexler. He did not want to be part of a rebuilding program; he wanted a chance to win before he retired. And if he were to be traded, he would like it to be to a contender.

But there was no deal at the beginning of the season; Clyde Drexler was still a Trail Blazer. And, acting as professionally as always, he gave it his all, averaging over 20.0 points per game for the Blazers during the first half of the season. As the season wore on, however, he became more anxious about a deal to the point of having his agent demand a trade. "I'd played myself out of there," said Drexler. "I'd seen transition in that organization quite a few times while I was there. But it wasn't only the rebuilding phase. It just wasn't going to work."

In response, Portland management asked if there was any place he wanted to go. "I'd like to go to Houston," Drexler responded, knowing that where he wanted to go and where he would end up probably would not be the same. "I just didn't think it was possible."

But then came that memorable Valentine's Day of 1995 when the Trail Blazers announced the trade that sent Drexler back to his hometown to play for the Rockets. "You're never too old to get excited," a very happy Drexler said after the trade. "Houston was just the icing on the cake."

He was appreciative of Portland accommodating him and gracious to his former club after the trade. "I have no ill feelings toward anyone in the Portland organization," Drexler said. "I thank them for the opportunity to play for them for 11½ years."

With players such as Olajuwon, Robert Horry, Kenny Smith, and Sam Cassell as teammates, Drexler's role with the Rockets would be different. "I've been concentrating on defense, passing the ball and just rebounding," he said after joining the Rockets. "On this team, it's not necessary that I score 20-25 points a game. This is a great team and a great system. We have a lot of people who can shoot the ball. So if they double-team, we're going to try and make them pay. I'll play both guard positions. Maybe some forward. Whatever Coach Tomjanovich designates, that's what I'll do."

Soon after the trade, the Rockets visited the White House where, as reigning NBA champs, they were met by President Clinton. Drexler, though he was traveling with the team, did not attend. "I'd feel like an impostor," he said. "Those guys deserve it. They had a great year last year. Hopefully, I'll join them next year."

But things went sour for the Rockets in March. Injuries plagued the club and it looked as if they did not have the strength to carry them through the second season. The Rockets, as a team, were struggling, but Drexler was playing outstanding basketball. In a game against the Dallas Mavericks, Drexler scored 41 points, while in another against the Los Angeles Clippers, he scored 40. For his work, he was named Player of the Week for the period ending April 9.

Maybe it was the home cooking at Drexler's Barbecue, the restaurant owned by Clyde's brother, James. Or maybe it was just being back in Houston, with his friends and family. Whatever the reason, the trade had rejuvenated Drexler.

Houston Rocket fans celebrate the back-to-back championships in 1995.

His mother was especially glad to have him home. "Just between himself and myself, he always said he wanted to come back," Eunice Drexler Scott said. "It feels good knowing he wanted to come home."

He was also greeted warmly by the hometown fans. In March, television ratings for Rockets' games jumped 15 percent and sellouts at the Summit became an everyday event. Clyde's return also spurred sales at Drexler's Barbecue, where Clyde once bussed tables. "Business is up maybe 30 percent," said Clyde's mother. The wait for ribs and chicken went from just five minutes the previous year, when the Rockets were playing the Knicks in the NBA Finals, to almost 30 minutes now that the prodigal son had come back home.

But with his return came the added pressure to win. And even though the Rockets were defending champs, with all their injuries and inconsistent play during the season no one gave them much of a chance to repeat.

In the first round, the Rockets had to take on the Utah Jazz, who, with John Stockton and Karl Malone, had won 60 games during the season and were ranked second in the Western Conference. The series was a best of five with the first two games to be played in Salt Lake City. In game one, Stockton scored on a drive with only a few seconds remaining to give the Jazz a 102-100 win. Game two was a different story. The Rockets routed the Jazz 140-126 with Drexler scoring 30 points and Rocket guard Kenny Smith 32.

The series continued in Houston for the third and fourth games. In the third game, Utah won 95-92. The Jazz were up 2-1 and now needed only one more victory to win the series. But the former "Phi Slama Jama" brothers from the University of Houston wouldn't let that happen. In game four, Olajuwon scored 40 and Drexler added 41 as the Rockets won easily, 123-106. "I think the feeling is finally setting in that when it gets close, we now have two guys to go to," Drexler said after the victory.

The fifth and deciding game was to be played in front of a screaming sellout crowd at the Delta Center in Salt Lake City. The game was close throughout, but the Rockets held the lead. With 6.5 seconds left in the game, Karl Malone connected on a three-point shot to bring the Jazz within two. But Drexler, who ended up scoring 31 points, hit three of four foul shots to give the Rockets a 95-91 victory and a first round series win. "We traded for an established player. We got professionalism, leadership, scoring. All of those qualities showed today," said Hakeem Olajuwon of Clyde Drexler after the game.

In the second round, this time a best of seven series, the Rockets were pitted against Charles Barkley and the Phoenix Suns. Again, they had to play the first two games on the road and this time the Rockets lost both. Down 0-2, they recovered in Houston to win game three 118-85, but the Suns beat them on their home court in game four.

With the Suns having to win only one more game to capture the series, and two of those to be played in Phoenix, things looked bleak for the Rockets. They got even bleaker when Drexler came down with the flu before game five. Though he made the effort to play, Drexler was obviously weakened and Coach Tomjanovich played him only sparingly. Still, the Rockets showed their character and squeaked out a 103-97 win. Back in Houston, the Rockets took game six 116-103 to tie the series. The deciding seventh game would be played in Phoenix. To win, the Rockets had to do it again in enemy territory.

It was a classic, see-saw battle and, appropriately, with less than a minute left, the score was tied. But with under 15 seconds to play, Mario Elie bombed a three-pointer to seal the victory for the Rockets. Next was the Western Conference Finals against the David Robinson-led San Antonio Spurs.

As had been the pattern in all the playoff series, the first two games were on the road. But this time the Rockets won both in San Antonio and then, inexplicably, lost two in a row at home. The series was tied going back to San Antonio for game five. Winning on the road was becoming a habit for the Rockets and game five was no different. Houston won 111-90 and gained and 3-2 edge in the series.

Back at the Summit in Houston, the Rockets closed out the Spurs in six, winning 100-95. They were Western Conference champs and were returning to the NBA finals for the second year in a row. But this time they were doing it with Clyde Drexler.

After the thrilling first three playoff series, the world was expecting another nail-biting series. But it was not to be. After beating the Magic in Orlando in the first game and taking away their spirit—and home-court advantage—the Rockets went on to win the next three, completing a clean sweep. In beating the Magic and repeating as NBA champs, the Rockets also set many playoff records. They became the first team to beat four 50-win teams in the playoffs; the first to win as many as nine playoff road games; and the first sixth seed to win it all. "This was a lesson not only for our team, but for people around the world to see how you can build character through hard work and by believing in one another," said the Rockets' leader, Hakeem Olajuwon.

Olajuwon averaged 33 points, 11.5 rebounds, and 5.5 assists per game in the finals and was named the series' MVP. The Dream definitely deserved the honor, but the next best player on court was Olajuwon's former college teammate, Clyde Drexler. In the series, he averaged 21 points and almost 10 rebounds per game.

After the thrilling first three playoff series, the Rockets four-game sweep of the Magic to win the championship was almost a letdown. But not to Drexler. It was a feeling he would never forget and his contributions were enormous. In the series he averaged 21 points and almost 10 rebounds per game. The only better player on the court was the series MVP, Hakeem Olaju-won.

That the two best players were former University of Houston teammates and good friends made the victory even sweeter. It had been 12 years since the two players watched as North Carolina State stunned them in the NCAA Championship Game. Now, finally, they could erase that hurt. After the clinching game, Drexler hugged Hakeem and said, with relief, "Twelve years later, huh?"

Winning two championships in a row was difficult enough, winning three seemed almost impossible. Yet that was the goal of the Houston Rockets for the 1995-96 season. Once again, however, the injury bug hit the Rockets. Drexler started off strong, but an ankle injury plagued

After defeating the Orlando Magic four games to none, Drexler walks off the court, finally showing that he is indeed a winner.

him all season and he ended up playing in only 52 games. Still, he was voted as a starter in the All-Star game in San Antonio and finished the year with a 19.3 scoring average.

Drexler was not the only one hit by injuries. At times it seemed as if the Rockets were made up of players from the Continental Basketball

Association (CBA). "The injury bug is a part of the game and you have to deal with it," Drexler said. "I think the frame of mind of this team is the most important thing, and I think there's not anyone here who believes that we can't do the same thing we did last season."

Before the playoffs were to begin, Drexler, in continuing his involvement with community affairs, was named League spokesman for the NBA in a joint effort with the National Committee to Prevent Child Abuse (NCPCA). Karl Malone of the Utah Jazz had held that title the year before Drexler.

"Clyde has a long-standing relationship with the NCPCA," said Anne Cohn Donnelly, executive director of the NCPCA. "While a member of the Portland Trail Blazers, he was actively involved with the local chapter. We are delighted he will continue his efforts this year on a national level."

The first round of the playoffs seemed a mirror of the previous year's. The Rockets met the Lakers and took them in five. But when they went up against the Seattle SuperSonics, the team with the best record in the Western Conference, and a younger, quicker team, the bubble finally burst. The Sonics beat the Rockets in a four-game sweep, ending Houston's two-year reign as champions. The Sonics went on to lose to the Chicago Bulls, a newly revitalized team with the return of Michael Jordan and the new addition of Dennis Rodman.

In 1997, Drexler again helped his team go deep into the NBA playoffs. During the regular season, he averaged 18 points and six rebounds per game as the Rockets won 57 games, finishing second in the Midwest Division. Houston reached the semifinals of the NBA playoffs, defeating Minnesota and Seattle in the first two rounds, but the Utah Jazz ended their season in six games.

With numerous awards behind him, and at the age of 33, Drexler seemingly has accomplished everything in basketball. He has won an NBA championship, was part of an Olympic Gold Medal team, participated in college basketball's Final Four, and played in 11 All-Star games. There is nothing more for him to prove. The debate is over. The case closed. History will rank him as one of the elite basketball players of his time.

STATISTICS

CLYDE DREXLER

University of Houston

Year	Games	Rebounds	Assists	Total Pts	Scoring Avg
1980-81	30	314	78	356	11.9
1981-82	32	336	96	485	15.2
1982-83	34	298	129	542	15.2

NBA-Portland

Year	Games	Rebounds	Assists	Total Pts	Scoring Avg
1983-84	82	235	153	628	7.7
1984-85	80	476	441	1,377	17.2
1985-86	75	421	600	1,389	18.5
1986-87	82	518	566	1,782	21.7
1987-88	81	533	467	2,185	27.0
1988-89	78	615	450	2,123	27.2
1989-90	73	507	432	1,703	23.3
1990-91	82	546	493	1,767	21.5
1991-92	76	500	512	1,903	25.0
1992-93	49	309	278	976	19.9
1993-94	68	445	333	1,303	19.2

Portland/Houston

Year	Games	Rebounds	Assists	Total Pts	Scoring Avg
1994-95	76	480	362	1,653	21.8

Houston

Year	Games	Rebounds	Assists	Total Pts	Scoring Avg
1995-96	52	373	302	1,004	19.3
1996-97	62	373	354	1114	18.0

Houston Rockets: 1995-NBA Champions
NBA All Star: 1986, 1988, 1989, 1990, 1991, 1992, 1993, 1994, 1996

CLYDE DREXLER
A CHRONOLOGY

1962   Born in Houston, Texas

1980   Enrolls at the University of Houston

1982   Helps lead the Cougars to a Cinderella appearance in the NCAA Tournament's Final Four

1983   Along with newcomer Hakeem Olajuwon, Drexler helps take the University of Houston to the NCAA championship game, where they lose on a last-second shot to North Carolina State; is drafted by the Portland Trail Blazers

1986   Plays in his first All-Star team

1987   Sets team record for most points scored

1990   Leads the Trail Blazers to the NBA championship series, where they lose to the Detroit Pistons

1992   Again leads the Trail Blazers to the NBA championship series, where they lose to the Chicago Bulls; wins a gold medal at the Olympics as a member of Dream Team II

1995   Is traded to the Houston Rockets and reunited with Hakeem Olajuwon; helps lead the Rockets to their second championship season, as they defeat the Orlando Magic in four straight games

SUGGESTIONS FOR FURTHER READING

Bloom, Barry, "Clyde Drexler." *Sport Magazine*, June 1995.

Bloom, Barry. "Dream Fulfilled." *Sport Magazine*, November 1995.

MacMullan, Jackie. "Clyde in Overglide." *Sports Illustrated*, February 1996.

ABOUT THE AUTHOR

J. Kelly is a prolific freelance writer who specializes in writing about sports, travel, and food. He is the author of Chelsea House's *Superstars of Women's Basketball*. He lives in New York City.

PICTURE CREDITS: AP/Wide World Photos: 2, 8, 11, 22, 24, 27, 33, 34, 36, 41, 42, 44, 47, 52, 55, 56, 60; Alameda Journal: 12, 17, 19; courtesy University of California, Berkeley: 29.

INDEX